I0415876

THE SECRETARY OF THE NAVY

SECNAV M-5214.1
DECEMBER 2005

DEPARTMENT OF THE NAVY

INFORMATION REQUIREMENTS (REPORTS) MANUAL

PUBLISHED BY
THE DEPARTMENT OF THE NAVY CHIEF INFORMATION OFFICER

DEPARTMENT OF THE NAVY

OFFICE OF THE CHIEF INFORMATION OFFICER
1000 NAVY PENTAGON
WASHINGTON, DC 20350-1000

31 December 2005

FOREWORD

This manual implements the policy set forth in Secretary of the Navy Instruction (SECNAVINST) 5210.16, *Department of the Navy (DON) Forms Management and Information Requirements (Reports) Management Programs*, 31 December 2005 regarding information collections (reports) and is issued under the authority of SECNAVINST 5430.7N, *Assignment of Responsibilities and Authorities in the Office of the Secretary of the Navy*, 9 June 2005. SECNAVINST 5214.2B, *Department of the Navy (DON) Information requirements (Reports) Management Program*, 6 December 1988 was cancelled by separate administrative action.

This Manual provides guidance to program managers and action officers who need to obtain information from the public, other Federal agencies, and within the DON and provides them with the procedures necessary to license their information requirements. It also provides guidance to assist information management control managers on the operation of their information collection programs.

This Manual is effective immediately; it is mandatory and applicable to the Offices of the Secretary of the Navy, The Chief of Naval Operations (CNO), the Commandant of the Marine Corps (CMC), and all Navy and Marine Corps activities, installations, and commands.

This manual may be accessed through the Department of the Navy, Navy Electronic Directives System website: http://neds.daps.dla.mil/. For further assistance or to offer comments and recommendation concerning this manual, contact the offices delineated below:

Office of the Secretary
and Navy Information
Management Control Officer
(CNO/DNS-5)
720 Kennon St. SE
Bldg 36 Room203
Washington DC 20374

Commercial:(202)433-2835
DSN: 288-2835

Marine Corps Information
Management Control
Officer(ARDB)
HQMC
2 Navy Annex
Washington DC 20380-1775

Commercial:(703)614-2311
DSN: 224-2311

D. M. Wennergren
Department of the Navy
Chief Information Officer

Department of the Navy
Information Requirements (Reports) Management Manual

Table Of Contents

FIGURES

REFERENCES

(a) Title 44 United States Code (USC), Chapters 21, 29, 31, and 33

(b) Title 44 USC Chapter 35, "Paperwork Reduction Act of 1995"

(c) Title 5 USC Chapter 5 § 552a, "Records Maintained on Individuals"

(d) Title 10 USC Chapter 88 § 1782, "Surveys of Military Families"

(e) Title 5 Code of Federal Regulations (CFR) Part 1320, "Controlling Paperwork Burdens of the Public"

(f) Title 41 Federal Management Regulations (FMR) Part 102-193, "Creation, Maintenance, and Use of Records"

(g) Title 41 FMR Part 102-194, "Standard and Optional Forms Management Program"

(h) Office of Management and Budget Circular A-130, "Management of Federal Information Resources"

(i) DOD 8910.1-M, "DOD Procedures for Management of Information Requirements," June 30, 1998, authorized by DODD 8910.1, "Management and Control of Information Requirements," June 11, 1993

(j) DODD 5230.9, "Clearance of DOD Information for Public Release," April 9, 1996

(k) DOD 5400.11-R, "Department of Defense Privacy Program," August 31, 1983, authorized by DODD 5400.11, "DOD Privacy Program," November 16, 2004

(l) DOD 7750.7-M, "DOD Forms Management Program Procedures Manual," August 1991, authorized by DODI 7750.7, "DOD Forms Management Program," May 31, 1990

(m) DODD 8320.2, "Data Sharing in a Net Centric Department of Defense," December 2, 2004

(n) DODI 1100.13, "Surveys of DOD Personnel," November 21, 1996

(o) DOD 8910.1-L, "Listing of Approved Recurring Information Requirements," updated monthly, authorized by DODD 8910.1, "Management and Control of Information Requirements," June 11, 1993

(p) DOD 4525.8-M, "DOD Official Mail Manual," December 2001, authorized by DODI 4525.8, "DOD Official Mail Management," December 26, 2001

(q) DODD 5200.27, "Acquisition of Information Concerning Persons and Organizations Not Affiliated with the Department of Defense," January 7, 1980

PART I

INTRODUCTION

1. <u>Purpose</u>. The purpose of this manual is to identify and provide procedures for the areas that comprise the DON Information Requirements (Reports) Program. Separate chapters cover internal information collections, public information collections, and interagency information collections.

2. <u>Background</u>. Information is vital to the success of any organization and provides the basis for management decisions. Specific types of data are needed to meet particular requirements. Information collections are the major means for providing this data. Information collections management encompasses the development of collections and information systems. As conditions or needs change, information management must provide for improvement of collections or systems; it must also provide for the control of information requirements to ensure minimum collection burden is expended and maximum effectiveness obtained.

3. <u>Philosophy And Scope</u>

   a. Leaders and managers require and expect organizations to furnish information necessary for effective performance of their mission.

   b. Information collections management consists of:

      (1) Information Control: The review and control of individual information collections to ensure efficient response to management requirements.

      (2) Information Collection Analysis: The development or improvement of collections and information systems.

   c. Increasingly, information collection is accomplished electronically. In particular, web based collections often provide a rapid, secure, and convenient means of collecting information.

4. <u>Definitions</u>

   a. <u>Administrative Issuances</u>. All instructions, notices, and change transmittals; administrative publications and manuals; general messages; and messages and correspondence containing material of a directive nature.

   b. <u>Agency</u>. Any executive department, Military Department, Government corporation, Government controlled corporation, or

other establishment in the executive branch of the Government
(including the Executive Office of the President), or any
independent regulatory agency, but does not include the General
Accounting Office, Federal Election Commission, the governments
of the District of Columbia and of the territories and
possessions of the United States, and their various
subdivisions, or Government-owned contractor-operated facilities
including laboratories engaged in national defense research and
production activities.

    c. As Required Report. Information collected, stored,
retrieved, and submitted when requested.

    d. Burden. The time, effort, or financial resources
expended by persons to provide information to a Federal agency.

    e. Collection of Information. Obtaining or soliciting facts
or by written report forms, application forms, schedules,
questionnaires, reporting or recordkeeping requirements, or
other similar methods calling for either:

        (1) Answers to identical questions posed to, or
identical reporting or recordkeeping requirements imposed upon,
ten or more persons, other than agencies, instrumentalities, or
employees of the United States.

        (2) Answers to questions posed to agencies,
instrumentalities, or employees of the United States, which are
to be used for general statistical purposes.

    f. Computer Generated Reports. Reports generated by
processing data residing in a computerized database.

    g. Exempt Information Collections. Information collections
that are exempt from the procedures in this manual.

    h. Information Collection (Report). Data or information
collected for use in determining policy; planning; controlling
and evaluating operations and performance; making administrative
determinations; or preparing other reports. The data or
information may be in narrative, statistical, graphic, or any
other form and may be displayed on paper, magnetic tape, or
other media.

    i. Information Collection Request. A written report form,
application form, schedule, questionnaire, reporting or recordkeeping requirement, or other similar method calling for the
collection of information.

    j. Information Requirement. The functional area expression
of need for data or information to carry out specified and
authorized functions or management purposes that require the
establishment of maintenance of forms or formats, or information
management collection or record keeping systems, manual or
automated.

    k. <u>Interagency Information Collection (Reporting) Requirement</u>. Any requirement involving submission of an information collection to an agency from one or more other agencies.

    l. <u>Internal Information Collection</u>. An information collection that remains within one organizational structure for its own use.

    m. <u>Licensed Information Collection</u>. An information collection that has been requested and justified by an action officer, reviewed and approved by the Command Information Management Control Manager, and assigned a Report Control Symbol or an exemption authority.

    n. <u>One-Time Information Collection</u>. An information collection prepared only once. One-time collections will be assigned a Report Control Symbol per SSIC code using "OT" as suffix number.

    o. <u>Operating Forces</u>. The activities comprising the operating forces of the Navy and the operating forces of the Marine Corps are listed in SNDL Part 1.

    p. <u>Recurring Information Collection</u>. An information collection that conveys essentially the same type of information at prescribed intervals.

    q. <u>Report Control Symbol (RCS)</u>. An organization abbreviation combined with a Standard Subject Identification Code (SSIC) (see SECNAV Manual M-5210.2) and a numeric suffix, which signifies that an information collection has been approved.

    r. <u>Revised Information Requirement</u>. An established information requirement that changes. The Information Management Control Manager must approve such revisions.

    s. <u>Shore Establishment</u>. The activities comprising the shore activities of the Navy and the Marine Corps are listed in SNDL Part 2.

    t. <u>Situation Information Collection</u>. An information collection which is prepared upon occurrence of a specified event.

    u. <u>Status Information Collection</u>. An interim information collection explaining the amount of work completed or to be completed on an established information collection.

    v. <u>Survey Or Personnel Survey</u>. An organized effort to obtain information from persons about themselves, their attitudes, perceptions, beliefs, opinions, or interests where the acquisition of such information is not a normal administrative requirement internal to the command.

    w. <u>Person</u>. An individual, partnership, association, corpo-ration, business trust, or legal representative, an organized group of individuals, a State, territorial, or local government or branch, or a political subdivision of a State, territorial, or local government or a branch of a political subdivision.

    x. <u>Unlicensed Information Collection</u>. An information collection that has <u>not</u> been sufficiently justified by the action officer, reviewed and approved by the Information Control Manager, and <u>not</u> assigned a Report Control Symbol or an exemption authority.

PART II

INFORMATION COLLECTIONS CONTROL

1. Responsibilities. Command Information Management Control Managers:

    a. Review information collections for conformance with reporting standards.

    b. Approve information collections by assigning report control symbols (RCS) or citing an appropriate exemption authority.

    c. Review individual information collections at least every three years.

    d. Maintain management data on information collections required by the organization (i.e., RCS, title of collection, purpose, cost, respondents, etc).

2. Clearance Procedures

    a. The action officer (originator of a proposed information collection) will submit all information concerning the information requirement to the Command Information Management Control Manager for approval. Information collections will be approved only when they comply with the procedures contained in this manual.

    b. The Command Information Management Control Manager should provide any assistance necessary to the action officer with the information requirement. This assistance is most effective when provided during the initial establishment of the information collection.

3. Follow-Up Procedures. Information collections will be reviewed to determine if they continue to meet requirements efficiently. The action officer will review the collection 180 days prior to the expiration of the information collection. Information collections not approved for extension are AUTOMATICALLY CANCELLED on the date of expiration and will be omitted from any subsequent effective collections listing. Collections without expiration dates are automatically cancelled after three years from date of approval.

4. Information Requirement Revalidation/Cancellation Procedures

    a. If an information requirement should be cancelled, prepare a change transmittal to the existing directive canceling the requirement. Submit a justification for the cancellation to the Information Management Control Manager.

   b. If the information requirement remains valid, submit a revised directive or change transmittal, within 60 days of the expiration date, explaining the revalidation and extending the approval period for a maximum period of an additional three years (see Figure 1). Also, prepare and submit a new Reports Analysis Data Form (see Figures 2 and 3).

DEPARTMENT OF THE NAVY
OFFICE OF THE CHIEF OF NAVAL OPERATIONS
WASHINGTON D.C. 20350

IN REPLY REFER TO

OPNAVINST 5200.19D CH-1
OP-945

OPNAV INSTRUCTION 5200.19D CHANGE TRANSMITTAL 1

From: Chief of Naval Operations

Subj: REVIEW, CLEARANCE, AND APPROVAL OF PROPOSED
        ADMINISTRATIVE ISSUANCES

1. Purpose. To revalidate the reporting requirement and extend
the reporting date in the basic instruction.

2. Validation and Approval of Extended Reporting Requirement
We use the information from this report to extract/obtain management
data for the reports control program, to document costs, to aid
in validating reporting requirements and assist in preventing
duplication. To control and reduce the burden placed on the operating forces and the shore establishment, we must extend the report
control symbol OPNAV 5214-1. We are approving the report contained
in the basic instruction for an additional three years.

3. Action. Add the following sentence to the report(s) paragraph:
Extend the reporting requirement contained in this directive until
(insert a month and year not greater than three years from the
date of the change transmittal).

Distribution:
(Same as basic)

Stocked:
CO, NAVY IFORMCEN
5801   Ave.
Philadelphia, PA 19120-5099

NOTES TO ORIGINATORS

Subject Line: Type in the subject of your basic in.

Paragraph 2:   State the reason for continuation of the report.

Figure 1. Sample Change Transmittal

RLS OPNAV 5214.1

REPORT ANALYSIS DATA

1. SSIC NUMBER	2. REPORT CONTROL SYMBOL

3. TITLE OF REPORT

4. PURPOSE OF REPORT

5. REQUIRING DIRECTIVE(S) (List of all that apply)

6. FREQUENCY OF REPORT
- [ ] DAILY
- [ ] QUARTE
- [ ] ONE TIME
- [ ] WEEKLY
- [ ] SEMIANNUAL
- [ ] SITUATIONAL
- [ ] MONTHLY
- [ ] ANNUALLY
- [ ] _____

7. REPORT FORMAT
- [ ] MESSAGE
- [ ] LETTER
- [ ] FORM (Attach copy)

8. IS REPORT SUBJECT TO MINIMIZE
- [ ] YES
- [ ] NO
- [ ] NOT APPLICABLE

9. METHOD OF PREPARATION
- [ ] ADPE
- [ ] TYPEWRITER
- [ ] MANUAL
- [ ] _____

10. IS REPORT ENTERED INTO AN ADP SYSTEM?
- [ ] NO
- [ ] YES (list name and location of system)

11. WHO USES COMPLETED REPORT? (List by command, OP code, sic.)

12. THIS REPORT IS COMPLETED BY [ ] OPERATING FORCES (SNDL Part I) [ ] SHORE ESTABLISHMENT (SNDL Part 2)

IF COMPLETED BY OPERATING FORCES, ARE FLEET CINC COMMENTS ATTACHED? [ ] YES [ ] NO

13. RESPONDENTS		OPERATING FORCES (SNDL Part I)	SHORE ESTABLISHMENT (SNDL Part 2)
	A. LIST RESPONDING COMMANDS BY A COLLECTIVE TERM OR BY NAME (FOR EXAMPLE FLTCINCS, TYCOMS, NAVAL LABS, ALL LEGSERVOFF, CRUITSTAS, AREA COORDINATORS, ALL OPER AVIATION SQUADRONS, ALL SUB-MARINES, ALL SSN, ALL SURFACE SHIPS, MAJOR CLAIMANTS, ALL SHOREACTS W/BEQ/BOQ, ALL COMDS W/DENTISTS, ALL S&S W/MEDPERS SYSCOMS, COMDS W/GEN MESS, ALL S&S, ALL COMDS W/CIVILIANS, ALL OVS COMDS, ALL ECHELON 2 COMDS)	(1)	(2)
	B. TOTAL NUMBER OF RESPONDENTS	(1)	(2)
	C. TOTAL COST TO PREPARE AND SUBMIT THIS REPORT (See reverse)	(1)	(2)

14. ACTION OFFICER	A. NAME, RANK/RATE/GRADE AND TITLE	B. ACTIVITY NAME AND ADDRESS (Include room number)	
	C. SIGNATURE	D. DATE	E. PHONE NO

OPNAV 5214/10 (REV 9-80)   S/N 0107-LF-052-1451

Figure 2. Report Analysis Data Form (OPNAV 5214/10)

Use this worksheet for estimating the total cost to prepare and submit this report. Compute two costs-one for operating forces and one for shore establishments. The hourly rate may be taken from any current pay chart.

OPERATING FORCES COSTS TO PREPARE AND SUBMIT

PAY GRADE	NO. HOURS SPENT	X HOURLY RATE	= PERSONNEL COSTS	+ 25% OVERHEAD	= TOTAL COSTS BY PAY GRADE		
			Total Cost of Prepare and Submit One report $ _____				
			X _____ Commands Required to Submit =			$ _____	
			X _____ Reports per Year			$ _____	
			Total Cost to Prepare and Submit			* $ _____	

*Enter this figure in column 13(c)(1)

SHORE ESTABLISHMENT COSTS TO PREPARE AND SUBMIT

PAY GRADE	NO. HOURS SPENT	X HOURLY RATE	= PERSONNEL COSTS	+ 25% OVERHEAD	= TOTAL COSTS BY PAY GRADE		
			Total Cost of Prepare and Submit One report $ _____				
			X _____ Commands Required to Submit =			$ _____	
			X _____ Reports per Year			$ _____	
			Total Costs to Prepare and Submit			** $ _____	

**Enter this figure in column 13(c)(2)

SAMPLE COMPUTATION (SALARIES ARE NOT ACCURATE)

PAY GRADE	NO. HOURS SPENT	X HOURLY RATE	= PERSONNEL COSTS	+ 25% OVERHEAD	= TOTAL COSTS BY PAY GRADE		
0-2 (Note 1)	.25	7.45	1.86	0.47			
E-8 (Note 2)	3	7.45	22.35	5.59			
GS-4 (Note 3)	1	4.77	4.77	1.19			
			Total Cost of Prepare and Submit One report $ 36.23				
			X 4 Commands Required to Submit =			$ 144.97	
			X 4 Reports per Year			$ 579.68	
			Total Costs to Prepare and Submit			$ 579.68	

Note 1: Reports and signs report
Note 2: Collects required information; prepares chart; writes report
Note 3: Types and mails report

OPNAV 5214/10 (REV. 9-81) (BACK)

Figure 3. Report Analysis Data Form (OPNAV 5214/10) (Back)

PART III

INFORMATION COLLECTIONS ANALYSIS

1. <u>General Criteria</u>. Information collections must provide a basis for measuring performance, making decisions, creating or revising policy, or carrying out operations and executing the mission of the organization establishing the information requirement.

   a. <u>Detailed Analysis</u>

      (1) Information collection items must be constructed to obtain all information needed concisely, economically, and effectively. Administrative issuances containing information requirements should be sufficiently clear to avoid misinterpretation.

      (2) Each item must satisfy a current need or known future requirement. The collection of information to meet a potential future need requires justification. The recipient of the information collection must use each reported item of information.

      (3) The validity of an information item can be determined by analyzing answers to the following questions:

         (a) Is the requested information under the cognizance of the requiring office?

         (b) Is the requested information necessary for an established objective?

         (c) How is the information used?

         (d) Could the information be obtained from some other source?

         (e) Is the information capable of misinterpretation? Could it be more simply stated?

         (f) Can the information be used for purposes other than the established objective? Are there other potential users of the information?

      (4) Negative response for information requirements and collections should only be required when they serve an established objective.

   b. <u>Arrangement of Information Management Collection Items</u>. Arrange collection data items in a logical format for easy completion by the preparing organization and for efficient use by the receiving organization. The organizational Information

Management Control Manager will assist in developing the most effective forms design.

    c. <u>Source of Information For Information Collection Items</u>. Determine the organization that can furnish precise, usable information in the easiest way. Reassignment of responsibility for preparation of information collections may avoid the establishment of unnecessary or duplicate source records, unnecessary workflow, or other uneconomical processes.

    d. <u>Controlling Copy Distribution</u>. Distribution of completed information management collections is based on a "need-to-act" or "need-to—know" basis. Distribution of courtesy copies is prohibited.

    e. <u>Timing Submissions</u>. Strive to minimize the collection burden by considering the timing and frequency of reporting. Take into account the following factors when considering timing:

    (1) <u>Minimum Frequency</u>. Establish the maximum time possible between collections.

    (2) <u>As Required Information Collections</u>. Establish these collections with the understanding that information will be available and furnished on request.

    (3) <u>Situation Information Collections</u>. These collections are required upon the occurrence of an event or situation or change in condition.

    (4) <u>Realistic Due Dates</u>. Allow sufficient time for adequate compilation between the end of the period covered and the due date.

    (5) <u>Peak Loads</u>. Stagger information collection submission dates to avoid conventional peak loads (e.g. end of the month and end of the quarter).

2. <u>Costing</u>

    a. <u>Need for costing</u>. Consider the cost of establishing new information requirements and of improving existing ones. Compare investment of work-hours and other costs to the value received from the information collection. Improved operations and effective decision-making processes, in some cases, justify costly collections and information systems.

    b. <u>Methods of estimating costs</u>. Base estimates on the actual situation. Estimate work hours and machine time from the approximate time spent by activity personnel to prepare and process the information. Obtain costs of any machine time, printing, special equipment, or other materials from the command requiring the information.

PART IV

INTERNAL INFORMATION COLLECTIONS

1. <u>Definitions</u>. See Part I, Section 3.

2. <u>Establishing An Information Requirement</u>

     a. Action officers establishing information requirements shall:

          (1) Prepare a Report Analysis Data Form (OPNAV 5214/10) for each information requirement contained in the administrative issuance establishing the information collection. (See Figure 2)

          (2) Ensure all requests from shore establishments for information requirements involving the operating forces are reviewed by the appropriate Fleet Commanders and that their comments are provided to the Information Management Control Manager.

          (3) Ensure information requirements are not authorized for longer than three years from the date of the administrative issuance establishing the information collection. A sentence must be included in the information collection paragraph stating that the information collection has been approved. Recurring information collections of less than three years will include the expiration date of the information collection in the information collections paragraph. One-time information collections, those submitted only one time, are not submitted or approved for three years.

          (4) Ensure justification of exemption is included as part of the information collection background material for exempt information collections. Include the identification of the exemption in the information collections paragraph (e.g., "The requirement contained in paragraph ___ is exempt from information collection control by SECNAVINST 5213.10E and requires no Report Control Symbol.")

          (5) Establish message information requirements when there is a clear operational requirement or time sensitive need only. If applicable, during periods of MINIMIZE (see paragraph 5.g.), ensure that the use of telecommunications to fulfill information requirements will be used by adding the words (MIN: CONSIDERED) after the Report Control Symbol.

          (6) Ensure respondents have sufficient time to collect, prepare, and transmit required information.

     b. After the above information has been compiled, the information collection sponsor will provide the following documents to the Information Management Control Manager for review and approval of the information collection:

       (1)   The proposed administrative issuance requiring the information collection.

       (2)   All references, enclosures, and cancelled documents, if any.

       (3)   All approved forms or formats.

       (4)   All necessary coordination and fleet commanders in chief comments, if applicable.

       (5)   Documentation exempting the information management collection from the control process, if applicable.

       (6)   Completed Report Analysis Data Form (OPNAV 5214/10). See figures 2 and 3.

   c. The Information Management Control Manager will review the documentation and decide if the information collection should be approved. The action officer will be notified of approval/disapproval. If the information collection was disapproved, an explanation will be provided.

3. <u>Filing Information Collection Material</u>

   a. <u>Case Folders</u>. Case folders will be maintained on all information collections established by the Command. Maintaining case folders on information collections prepared by the command for other activities are optional and at the discretion of the Information Management Control Manager.

   b. <u>Information Collection Case Folder</u>. Maintain case folders on each established information collection and include:

       (1)   A completed Report Analysis Data form (for non-exempt reports).

       (2)   A copy of the report form, format or a copy of the information collection.

       (3)   A copy of the document requiring the information collection.

   c. <u>Arrangement of Case Folders</u>. Arrange folders chronologically by Report Control Symbol.

4. <u>Information Collection (Reports) Control Inventory</u>. An accurate inventory of information collections (reports) is essential for effective operation and will be maintained by the Information Management Control Manager. Activities will maintain case folders on those information collections over which they have cognizance. The Reports Record Card (OPNAV 5214/5) (see

Figure 3) is available to assist Information Management Control Managers in establishing an inventory system. The purpose of the inventory is to provide:

   a. A central reference point for all information collections required by the activity.

   b. A source of information for comparison or background use in the review of new information collections and revisions to existing information collections.

   c. A source of information to avoid duplication of existing information requirements.

5. Report Control Symbols. A Report Control Symbol is assigned by the command Information Management Control Manager. SECNAV and OPNAV Report Control Symbols are assigned by OPNAV (DNS-51). USMC report Control Symbols are assigned by HQMC (ARDB).

   a. Necessity of Report Control Symbols. A Report Control Symbol indicates that the information collection has been reviewed and approved as a valid requirement and the respondents have the responsibility of providing the requested information.

   b. Use of Higher Authority Report Control Symbols. The symbol of the highest authority will appear on the information collection. For example, if a DD symbol is assigned to an information collection, all responding commands will use the DD symbol, expiration dates as assigned by the Office of the Secretary of Defense (OSD) and associated information collection title. Information Management Control Managers cannot substitute their command symbol to an information collection having a higher-level symbol.

   c. Unlicensed Reports. Organizations are not required to respond to unlicensed or expired reports.

   d. Composition of a Navy Report Control Symbol. The Information Management Control Manager assigns the symbols. An example is OPNAV 5214/5 (See Figure 4).

      (1) The letters OPNAV indicate the authorized abbreviation of the bureau, office, shore activity or fleet command requiring the information collection (OPNAV is the abbreviation for the Office of the Chief of Naval Operations).

      (2) The four or five digits together, 5213, indicate the DON Standard Subject Identification Codes (SSIC) number which identifies the subject of the report (5213 is Information Requirements (Reports) Management). Use SECNAV Manual M-5210.2 to find the appropriate SSIC numbers and their associated narrative subjects.

      (3) The last digit, separated by a dash, is the next consecutive number in that SSIC series. In the example, OPNAV

5213-1 is the first OPNAV symbolized information collection in the 5213 series.

(4) Consecutive numbers assigned in a Report Control Symbol cannot be reused even if the information collection is subsequently cancelled or expired.

e. Composition of A Department of Defense (DOD) Report Control Symbol. These symbols are assigned by the Washington Headquarters Services, Directorate for Information Operations and Reports (WHS/DIOR). An example of a DOD symbolized recurring information collection is DD-COMP(SA)725--Reimbursable Transactions.

(1) The letters DD indicate that this is a Department of Defense information collection.

(2) The abbreviation before the parenthesis is the office within DOD requiring the information collection (COMP is the office of the Comptroller).

(3) The letters in parenthesis indicate the frequency of the report (SA is semi-annual).

(4) The digits indicate the next consecutive number assigned by the DOD Information Management Control Officer for the overall system (725 is the next consecutive number assigned for all DOD reports; not the next consecutive number for COMP reports).

(5) The DON Information Management Control Manager assigns an appropriate SSIC number in parenthesis after the DOD symbol. For Navy purposes the Report Control Symbol DD-COMP (SA)725(7010) represents a DD information collection with the SSIC 7010 to designate an information collection on non-appropriated funds. The entire number is written without spaces.

(6) A one-time DOD Report Control Symbol is written as DD-COMP (OT)8836(7010). This is the same as the recurring Report Control Symbol except OT means the information collection will only he submitted one time. The first two digits, 88, indicate the calendar year the information collection was established and the next two digits, 36, reflect the next consecutive number for one time reports controlled for that year. The figure 8836 in the above example means that this is the 36th one-time report assigned in calendar year 1988.

f. Location of The Report Control Symbol In Documents

(1) When an administrative issuance establishes an information collection, cite the Report Control Symbol, title, paragraph establishing the requirement or the exemption authority in the last paragraph (above the signature) of the document imposing the information collection.

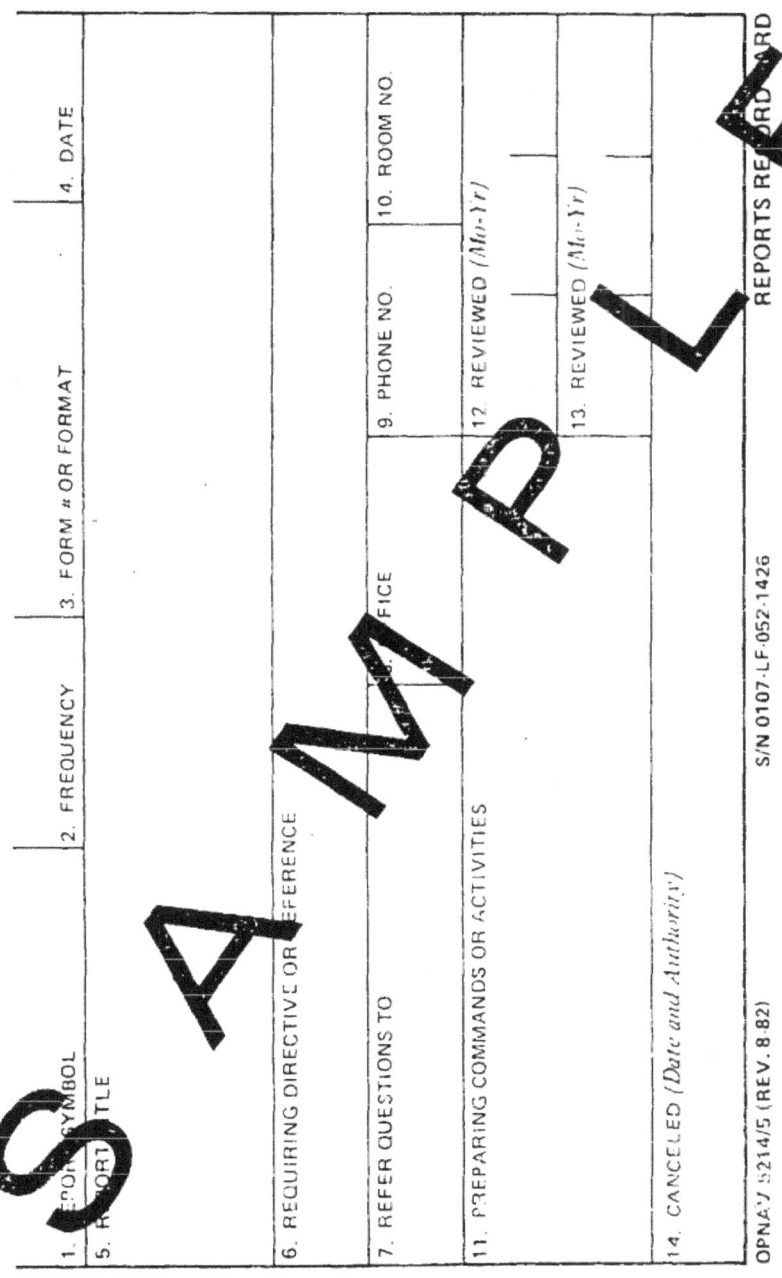

Figure 4. Report Record Card (OPNAV 5214/5)

(2)   When a document references an information collection that has been established by prior issuance, cite the Report Control Symbol in the same paragraph that mentions the information collection.

g.   MINIMIZE

(1)   When an actual or simulated emergency occurs, a reduction of telecommunications use may be necessary. This action is required to facilitate prompt transmission of essential traffic. Essential traffic is that which must be transmitted to avoid serious detrimental impact on mission accomplishment or safety of life. Commanders have the authority to impose MINIMIZE within their command or area of command responsibility unless specifically denied.

(2)   The information collection sponsor must determine if the information required is important enough to be received during MINIMIZE conditions.

(3)   When an information collection is to be transmitted during MINIMIZE conditions, the words (MIN:CONSIDERED) are written in parenthesis after the Report Control Symbol; for example, OPNAV 1000-1 (MIN:CONSIDERED).

(4)   Greater effort is required to enforce MINIMIZE. Therefore, all messages released during MINIMIZE will include as the last sentence "Released by" followed by the rank/grade and name of the releaser.

6.   Publishing Lists of Information Collections. Each organization should periodically publish a list of its current information collections (reports). Include the following for current information collections (reports):

a.   Report Control Symbol.

b.   Title of the information collection.

c.   Form number or format.

d.   Frequency of submission.

e.   Document requiring the information collection.

f.   The organization code sponsoring the information collection.

g.   Organizations that must respond to the information collection (collective terms preferred).

7.   Exemptions. The following subject matters are exempt from reports control:

a. Communications actions on declaration of war.

b. Establishment or cancellation of MINIMIZE.

c. Compromises of classified information.

d. Status changes for Communications Security Material System (CMS) items and cryptographic keying material.

e. Information concerning imminent danger to life, health, or property arising from dangerous or defective material.

f. Issuances establishing defense conditions or alerts of a service—wide nature.

g. Reports of events or special incidents that may attract national and/or high U.S. Navy interest.

h. Operational reports flowing within the Navy Command and Control System (NCCS) to support commanders in planning, directing, and controlling operations of assigned forces by assigned missions. Reports contained in communications tactical publications.

i. Substantive intelligence reporting.

j. Operating documents and information or documentation processed and/or transmitted within an operational system. Examples are application forms, purchase orders, bills of lading, personnel actions, payrolls and timesheets, and reports of inspections.

k. Report of findings, recommendations, or actions prepared by an official committee, board, study group, or task force.

l. Comments or concurrences which are part of the routine clearance of proposed actions or publications and recommendations or evaluations as to existing or proposed plans, policies, procedures, organizations, missions, publications, agenda, or courses of action.

m. Public information releases.

n. Reports of audits, internal reviews, investigation of charges, complaints, claim or violation of laws and regulations. Reports of internal reviews when imposed by a higher-level command are not exempt.

o. Counterintelligence, personnel security, and other investigative surveys and reports as covered by SECNAVINST 3820.2D.

p. Reports concerning personnel matters such as savings bond participation, conflict of interest statements, financial statements, nominations, and routine medical and dental documents.

    q. Routine requests for cost estimates related to a
specific information request.

PART V

PUBLIC INFORMATION COLLECTIONS

1. Definitions. See Part I, Section 3.

2. Objectives.

     a. Minimize the Federal and information collection burden for individuals, small businesses, state and local governments, and other persons.

     b. Minimize the cost to the federal government of collecting, maintaining, using, and disseminating information.

     c. Maximize the usefulness of information collected by the federal government.

3. Procedures

     a. Each request to collect information from the public must he approved by the Office of Management and Budget (OMB). To obtain this approval, the action officer of the request must include the report in the Information Collection Budget (ICB) submitted to OMB in July of each year. The ICB consists of all existing and new public information collections (reports), both recurring and one-time, that might be established during the year. Since requirements for submission of the ICB frequently change each year, action officers should notify the DON Forms Manager and the DON Information Management Control Manager (DNS-51) as soon as possible of any potential new public information collection in order to obtain guidance for including the collection in the ICB.

     b. When a new information collection is to be approved or an existing one extended, the action officer will submit the following completed documents, via the chain of command, to DNS-51:

          (1) Paperwork Reduction Act Submission (OMB Form 83-I). Instructions for completing this form are contained in OMB 83-I INST.

          (2) A supporting statement following the instructions provided in the OMB 83-I INST. The statement must clearly state the information requirement being requested.

          (3) The form, survey, questionnaire or collection form, and all privacy act statements.

          (4) Proposed instructions for completing the information collection, if any.

          (5) The information to be submitted for publication

in the Federal Register (a sample format may be obtained from DNS-51).

c. DNS-51 will submit the Information Collection Budget to the Washington Headquarters Services Directorate, Information Management Division for review and forwarding to OMB for final action.

d. The request originator will receive written notification of OMB's final action. If the information collection is approved, a Report Control Symbol and expiration date will be assigned to the information collection. The symbol must be used on all subsequent documentation concerning the information collection. If approval is not granted, the information may not be collected. Collecting information that has not been approved by OMB is a direct violation of Public Law 96-511.

4. <u>Composition of A Public Report Control Symbol</u>. These symbols, such as 0703-0003, are assigned by OMB.

a. The first four digits represent the number assigned to the agency requiring the report; for example, Air Force is 0701, Army is 0702, Navy is 0703, and OSD is 0704.

b. The last three digits represent the next consecutive number assigned to the requiring agency's approved public information collections. In the example above, 0003 is the third public reporting requirement approved for the Navy.

5. <u>Exemptions</u>. The following types of information collections from the public are exempt from OMB review:

a. Affidavits, oaths, affirmations, certification, receipts, changes of address, consents, or acknowledgments, provided that they entail no burden other than that necessary to identify the respondent, the date, the respondent's address, and the nature of the instrument

b. Samples of products or of any other physical objects

c. Facts or opinions obtained through direct observation by an employee or agent of the sponsoring agency or through non-standardized oral communication in connection with such direct observations

d. Facts or opinions submitted in response to general solicitations of comments from the public, published in the Federal Register or other publications, provided that no other person is required to supply specific information pertaining to the commenter, other than necessary for self-identification, as a condition to the agency's full consideration of the comment

e. Facts or opinions, obtained initially or in follow-up requests, from individuals (including individuals in control groups) under treatment or clinical examination in connection with research on, or prophylaxis to prevent, a clinical disorder; direct treatment of that disorder; or in the interpretation of biological analyses of body fluids, tissues, or other specimens; or the identification or classification of such specimens

    f. A request for facts or opinions addressed to a single person

    g. Examination designed to test the aptitude, abilities, or knowledge of the persons tested and the collection of information for identification or classification in connection with such examinations

    h. Facts or opinions obtained or solicited at or in connection with public hearings or meetings

    i. Facts or opinions obtained or solicited through non-standardized follow-up questions designed to clarify responses to approved collections of information

    j. Like items so designated by OMB

    k. Collections of information from federal employees within the scope of their employment, unless the results are to be used for general statistical purposes

    l. Members of the Armed Forces serving on active duty, members of their families, and retired members of the Armed Forces when being surveyed within the context of Section 804 of the FY 1986 Defense Authorization Act

    m. Collections of information from fewer than 10 persons

    n. Collections of information involving compulsory process under the Anti-Trust Civil Process Act, or Section 13 of the Federal Trade Commission Improvements Act of 1980

    o. Collections of information required during the conduct of intelligence activities, as defined in Section 4-206 of Executive Order 12036, issued January 24, 1978, or successor orders, including Executive Order 12333, issued December 4, 1981; or during the conduct of crypto-logic activities that are communications securities activities

    p. Public collections of information needed during the conduct of a federal criminal investigation or prosecution, during the disposition of a particular criminal matter, during the conduct of a civil action to which the United States or any official or agency thereof is a party, or during the conduct of an administrative action or investigation involving an agency against specific individuals or entities

PART VI

INTERAGENCY INFORMATION COLLECTIONS

1. <u>Definitions</u>. See Part I, Section 3.

2. <u>Objective</u>. To ensure that Navy interagency information collections collect only essential information to avoid duplication and needless expenditures.

3. <u>Procedures</u>

    a. If a new, revised or extended interagency information collection is required by a Department of Navy (DON) organization, locate the Office of Secretary of Defense (OSD) sponsor. The OSD sponsor will prepare and submit a Request for Approval of Information Collections (SD Form 455) to the DOD Internal Information Management Control Manager for review and approval. The Navy organization will provide the OSD sponsor with:

        (1) Cost estimate of the collection

        (2) The collection instrument and any instructions pertaining to it

        (3) A copy of the authority for collecting the information

    b. If the action officer's Information Management Control Manager concurs with the information requirement, forward the items listed above to DNS-51. After review, the information will be forwarded to the DOD Internal Information Management Control Officer for final action and, if approved, the assignment of an Interagency Report Control Number (IRCN).

    c. After final action by DOD Internal Information Management Control Manager, a copy of the SD Form 455 is returned to the sponsoring OSD activity. An approved interagency collection will contain the IRCN and expiration date. The IRCN and must appear in the DON issuing authority. If the interagency collection is disapproved, the information may not be collected.

4. <u>Composition of An Interagency Report Control Symbol</u>. These symbols, such as DD-P&R (AR)9999-I, are assigned by the DOD Information Management Control Officer.

    a. The first two letters indicate that DOD is collecting the information.

    b. The letter abbreviation is the OSD activity sponsoring the collection.

c. The remaining letters indicate the frequency of the submission of the information. AR equates to "As Required".

d. A sequential number will follow the frequency.

e. An "I" will follow the sequential number indicating the information collected from other federal agencies (i.e. interagency collection).

f. For DON purposes, an appropriate SSIC number is assigned in parenthesis after the IRCN (i.e., 5212). The IRCN cited above would become DD-P&R(AR)9999-I(5212) and is written without spaces.

PART VII

SELF INSPECTION GUIDE FOR INFORMATION MANAGEMENT CONTROL MANAGERS

1. <u>Objective</u>. This guide is designed to assist Information Management Control Managers in evaluating overall information collection management policies, standards, organizational structure, staffing, and procedures.

2. <u>Procedures</u>. Self-inspection ensures proper information collection management throughout an organization. The answers to the following questions should assist in evaluating program effectiveness:

    a. <u>Program Placement and Responsibilities</u>

        (1) Is the overall responsibility for information collections assigned at the executive level?

        (2) Is information collections management part of the overall records and information management program?

        (3) Does placement of the program allow for coordination among other Records Managers?

        (4) Have information collections management responsibilities been clearly delegated in writing?

    b. <u>Program Documentation</u>

        (1) Is there a current directive outlining information collections management policy, objectives, and responsibilities?

        (2) Are there written procedures for performing information collections management functions?

        (3) Does the information collections management directive include procedures for internal, interagency, and public reports?

        (4) Are there written procedures for ensuring compliance with the Privacy Act?

        (5) Are there written procedures for coordinating information requirements with ADP activities, and forms, directives, and other related elements?

        (6) Are information collections required to be analyzed for duplication and redundancy, and are there written procedures for doing so?

(7)   Is there a requirement for cost analysis of information collections?

(8)   Is there a stipulation that respondents will not comply with an information requirement unless the Report Control Symbol or exemption authority is provided?

(9)   Are information collections required to be checked for compliance with applicable laws, regulations and policies?

(10) Are automated information collections subject to the same reviews and controls as non—automated collections?

c.   Program Records

(1)   Does the office responsible for information collections management maintain a history (case) file with background information on each proposed and approved information collection?

(2)   Does the history file contain information on the purpose of the information collection, justification, originating office or official, implementing directive, related forms, and costing?

(3)   Does the information collections management office maintain a complete set of directives, rules, regulations, and internal procedural documents governing information collections?

(4)   Is a listing of effective information collections (reports)issued on at least an annual basis?

(5)   Is the listing of effective information collections current?

(6)   Are the information collections in the listing grouped by function, report symbol, or subject to avoid duplication?

d.   Program Operations

(1)   Does the information collections management staff provide training to sponsors on the need for information collections management and the sponsor's responsibilities?

(2)   Does the Information Collections Control Manager provide training and technical assistance in analyzing and determining information needs and system design?

(3)   Are procedures for information collections management available to be followed by persons who require, prepare, process, and use information collections?

(4)   Have practices that bypass the clearance process been eliminated (avoid unlicensed reports)?

(5)   Are waivers and exceptions to the clearance process properly documented and legitimate?

(6)   Do action officers coordinate proposed information collections with those who will be affected by them?

(7)   Is senior management aware of the number, types and costs of information collections and systems required by organization components?

(8)   Have directives outlining information requirements been distributed to responding organizations on a timely basis?

PART VIII

INFORMATION COLLECTIONS (REPORTS) EVALUATION GUIDE

1. <u>Objective</u>. This guide is designed to improve the evaluation of individual information collections (reports).

2. <u>Procedures</u>. The following questions should assist Information Management Control Managers in evaluating information collections:

    a. <u>Need and Use</u>

        (1) Is there a specified purpose for the information collection?

        (2) Is the information collection used to make a decision or take a specific action?

        (3) Would the performance of any function be impaired without the information collection?

        (4) Are all items on the information collection used?

        (5) Have all items falling into the "nice to know" category been eliminated?

        (6) Are all copies of the information collection used?

        (7) Are there any copies used strictly for informational purposes? If so, are they really necessary?

    b. <u>Adequacy and Suitability</u>

        (1) Is all data accurate and complete?

        (2) Does the data match the specific need of each user?

        (3) Is the information being reported valid and timely?

        (4) Has a one—time situation report been substituted for a periodic report when that would serve the purpose?

        (5) Is the data summarized whenever possible?

        (6) Does the information collection contain comparisons of data? (Collections that include comparative data are usually more useful than raw data or statistics.)

        (7) Have production or performance goals been set and

used to compare data?

        (8)   Are meaningful comparative bases used, such as established standards, past performance, financial or production goals, and correlations with other schedules, programs, or events?

        (9)   Are graphics, such as illustrations, charts, graphs, etc., used to good advantage?

        (10) Is the information collection style suitable for intended users (i.e., executives, technicians, the general public)?

        (11) Is the tone, or the presence or absence of detailed statistics, appropriate to the users' level of responsibility and knowledge?

        (12) If statistics are used, are they meaningful?

        (13) Does the complete information collection provide maximum simplicity and utility for the intended respondents and users?

    c.   Distribution of the Information Collection

        (1)   Is the method for distributing the information collection adequate?

        (2)   Has the accuracy of the distribution been verified in the last year?

        (3)   Is a copy of the information collection forwarded to everyone who needs and uses the information?

        (4)   Has consideration been given to broader distribution of the information collection instead of preparing summary reports?

    d.   Relationship to functions

        (1)   Is the information collection related to the user's functions?

        (2)   If the user's functions and responsibilities have recently changed, has the change been reflected in the information collection?

        (3)   Could another action eliminate an information collection?

    e.   Sources

        (1)   Is the information in the information collection obtained from the best source?

(2)   Has consideration been given to using the information available in a different form or from another organization (such as a computer printout)?

(3)   Are files or other sources maintained so that data can be easily extracted?

f.   Cost

(1)   Has a cost analysis been performed on the information collection?

(2)   Has costing information been documented?

(3)   Is data being obtained and processed in the least costly manner?

g.   Timing

(1)   Are information collection periods clearly stated in the implementing directive?

(2)   Is the information collection needed for a specific period of time only, and has it been assigned an expiration date consistent with that need?

(3)   Is the due date clearly stated?

(4)   Is the frequency (monthly, quarterly, annually) of the information collection specified?

(5)   Is the information collection frequency consistent with the users' needs?

(6)   Are deadlines realistic?

(7)   Have the heaviest workload periods, such as the end of a month or a quarter, been avoided if possible? Try to use 15th of the month and tri-annual information collection periods rather than peak periods.

h.   Sampling

(1)   Is complete coverage, rather than a sample, essential?

(2)   If sampling is used, is it representative enough to provide accurate data?

i.   Combination

(1)   Have all possibilities for combining the information collection with other reports been considered?

(2)   If automated, has the data been integrated with other systems or databases where possible?

(3)   Have the data needs of other offices been coordinated?

j.   Instructions

(1)   Are the information collection instructions sufficiently detailed and clear?

(2)   Do the instructions provide for standardized information collection?

k.   Report Control Symbol

(1)   Is the report appropriately licensed?

(2)   Is the Report Control Symbol shown on forms and records associated with the information collection to tie together the related forms and directives?

l.   Authentication

(1)   Are the signatures of verifying and approving officials required only when necessary?

(2)   Are the signatures at the appropriate level of authority?

m.   Format

(1)   Is the information collection format prescribed?

(2)   Do all preparing offices use the same format?

(3)   Has a form been used where appropriate?

(4)   Has a form that already exists been used for collecting required information where appropriate?

n.   Design

(1)   Is the text of fill—in information collection forms arranged to permit easy fill-in and use?

(2)   Is there adequate space for each item?

(3)   Are items in proper sequence according to the user's needs, especially when data is transferred from an information collection to an automated form?

(4)   Are recurring items, such as the recipient's address, preprinted on the information collection form whenever possible?

(5)   Are the instructions adequate and are they placed where they are readily seen; are they clear and descriptive; do the boxes, lines, type, etc, emphasize the captions?

(6)   If multiple copies of a form are required, is the form available electronically, or in sets using interleaved carbons or carbonless paper?

(7)   Is the size of the form adequate, practical, and easy to read; will it fit in standard files or binders?